# Gold Stars®

# Starting to Add

# PaRRagon

Bath • New York • Cologne • Melbourne • Delhi
Hong Kong • Shenzhen • Singapore • Amsterdam

D1514491

# Helping your child

⭐ Remember that the activities in this book should be enjoyed by your child. Try to find a quiet place to work.

⭐ Your child does not need to complete each page in one go. Always stop before your child grows tired, and come back to the same page another time.

⭐ It is important to work through the pages in the right order because the activities do get progressively more difficult.

⭐ The answers to the activities are on page 32.

⭐ Always give your child lots of encouragement and praise.

⭐ Remember that the gold stars are a reward for effort as well as for achievement.

This edition published by Parragon Books Ltd in 2014

Parragon Books Ltd
Chartist House
15–17 Trim Street
Bath BA1 1HA, UK
www.parragon.com

Illustrated by Simon Abbott
Written by David and Penny Glover
Educational consultant: Christine Vaughan

ISBN 978-1-4723-5685-7

Printed in China

# Contents

# Count 1, 2, 3

How many balloons can you count in each set?
Write the answers in the boxes.

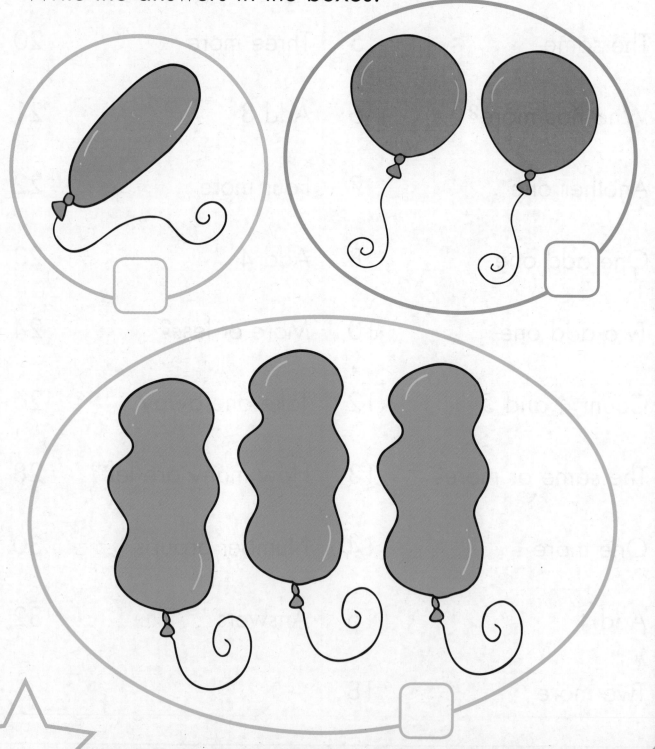

Note for parent: Children need to be confident with counting before they can start to add.

# The same

Count the spots on each shirt. Draw lines to join the T-shirts with the same number of spots.

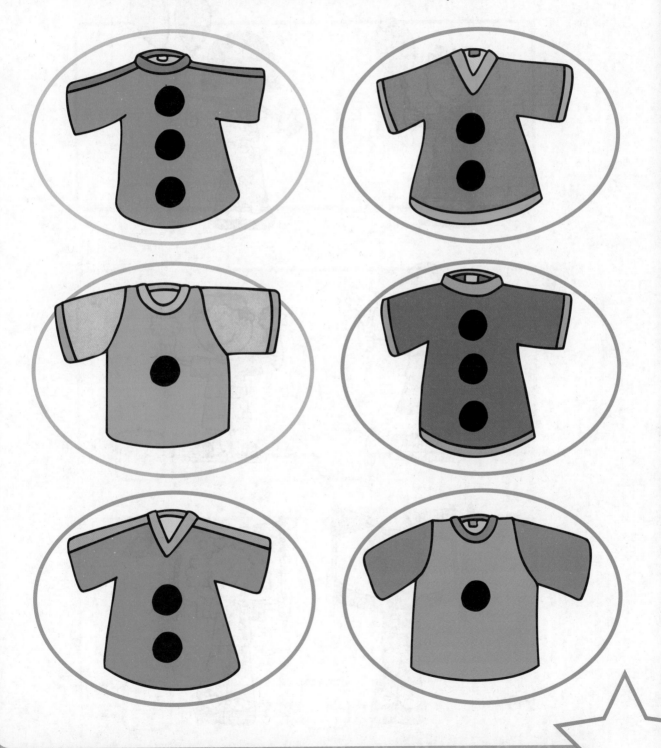

Note for parent: Identifying numbers that are the same or different prepares your child for adding and subtracting.

# Who has more?

Look at the pictures. Put a tick by the person in each row who has more.

Note for parent: This activity gives more practice in counting from 1 to 3 and introduces the idea of 'more' and 'less'.

# Another one

Each dog needs a ball. Draw 1 more.

Each child needs a cake. Draw 1 more.

Note for parent: Practise making numbers the same when you lay the table or share sweets.

7

# One add one

Point to each picture and count the objects.
Say the numbers out loud.

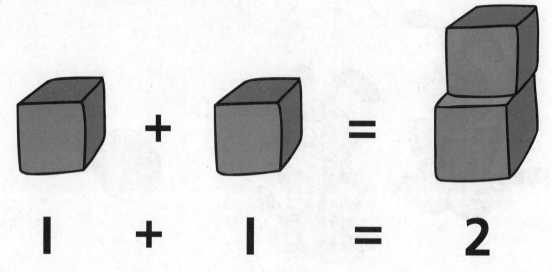

**1    +    1    =    2**

One and one make two.

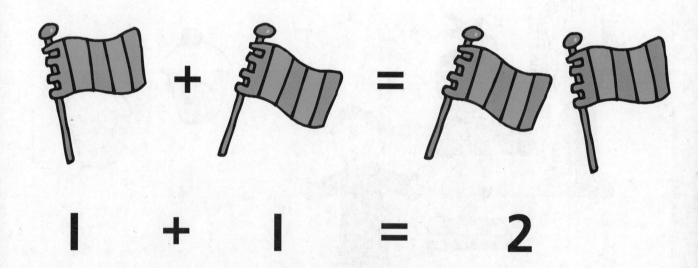

**1    +    1    =    2**

Write the numbers in the boxes to make the totals.

⭐ + ⭐ = ⭐⭐

1 + 1 = ☐

🏐 + 🏐 = 🏐🏐

1 + 1 = ☐

Point to each picture and count the objects.
Say the numbers out loud.

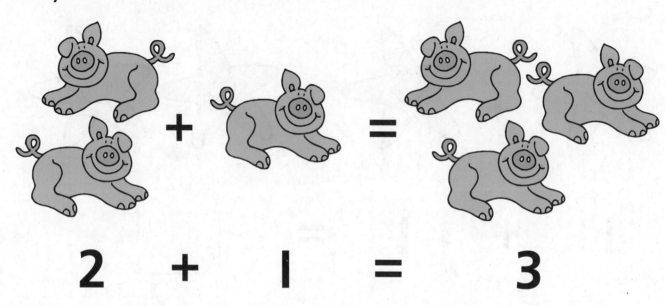

**2    +    1    =    3**

Two and one make three. Write the answer in the box.

**2    +    1    =**

Note for parent: Count the things on the left, then the things on the right. Are the numbers the same?

Colour the answers to these sums.

2 + 1 = 3

2 + 1 = 3

# Count 4 and 5

Colour four ducks.

Colour five fish.

Note for parent: Children often find it difficult to count objects that are not arranged in tidy rows: encourage them to cover up each one as they count it.

# The same or more?

Join each rabbit to a hole. Are there more rabbits or holes? Tick the correct box.

more rabbits ☐        more holes ☐

Draw lines to see if there are more dogs or kennels. Tick the correct box.

more kennels ☐        more dogs ☐

Note for parent: Matching objects one by one shows if the numbers are the same or different.

13

Colour one more flag.

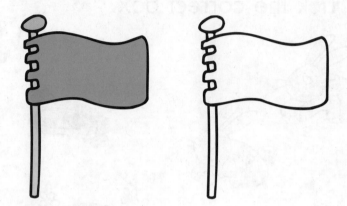

How many flags are there altogether?

Colour one more apple.

How many apples are there altogether?

Note for parent: Use a variety of words to talk about adding – add, and, plus, make, one more, another one, altogether, sum.

Colour one more butterfly.

How many butterflies are there altogether?

Colour one more hat.

How many hats are there altogether?

# Add 1

Point to each picture and count the objects.
Say the numbers out loud.

1 + 1 = 2

One and one make two.

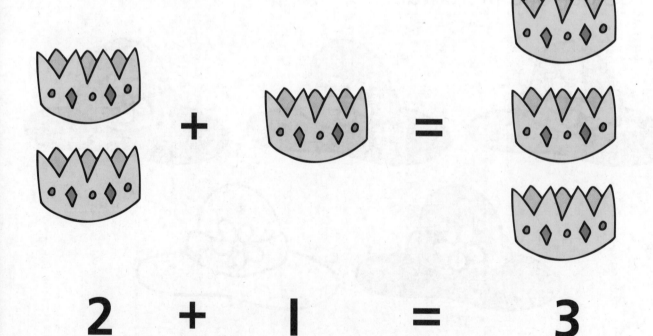

2 + 1 = 3

Note for parent: Count the objects in both pictures on the left with your child and point out that the last number in the count gives the total.

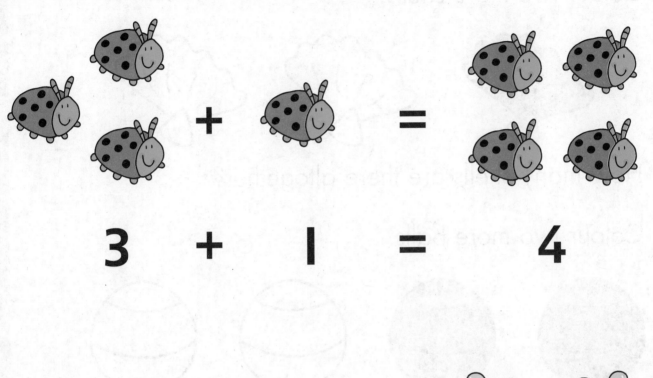

3     +     1     =     4

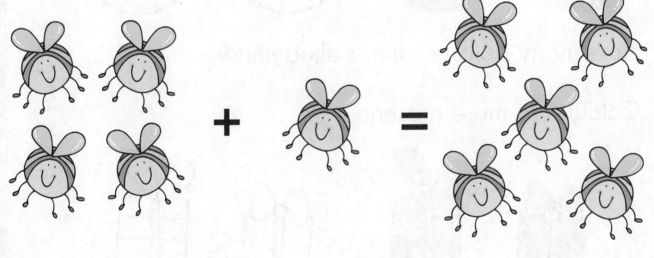

4     +     1     =     5

# Two more

Colour two more shells.

How many shells are there altogether?

Colour two more balls.

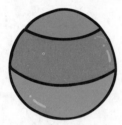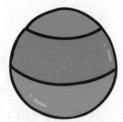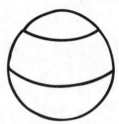

How many balls are there altogether?

Colour two more presents.

How many presents are there altogether?

Note for parent: In this activity your child is adding things or objects in groups.

# Add 2

Point to each picture and count the objects.
Say the numbers out loud.

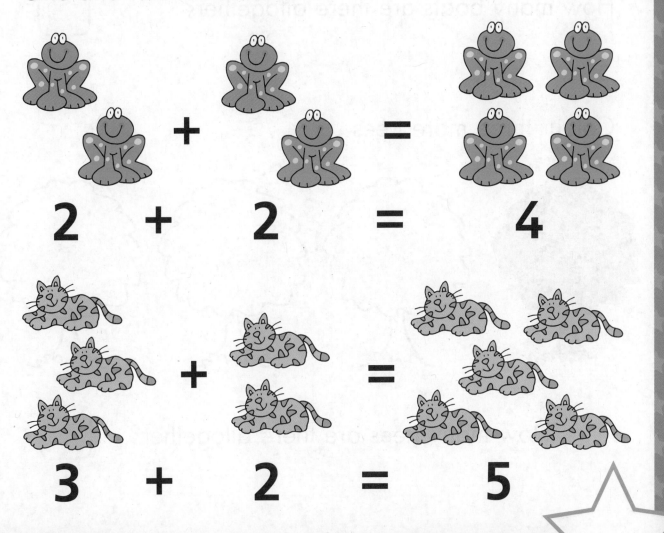

1 + 2 = 3

One and two make three.

2 + 2 = 4

3 + 2 = 5

Note for parent: Practise counting groups of everyday objects (with totals of up to 5) with your child.

Colour three more boats.

How many boats are there altogether?

Colour three more trees.

How many trees are there altogether?

Note for parent: Building brick towers is an excellent way to make number work fun.

# Add 3

Point to each picture and count the objects.
Say the numbers out loud.

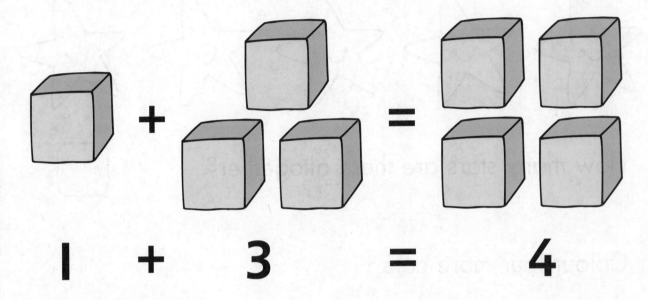

**1 + 3 = 4**

One and three make four.

**2 + 3 = 5**

# Four more

Colour four more stars.

How many stars are there altogether?

Colour four more cars.

How many cars are there altogether?

Note for parent: Encourage your child to use their fingers to count and add.

Point to each picture and count the objects.
Say the numbers out loud.

**1  +  4  =  5**

One and four make five.

**1  +  4  =  5**

Look at the pictures. Draw a line to join the two children with the same number of cakes.

Draw a ring around the child with the most cakes.

Note for parent: The idea of 'less' is needed to understand subtraction.

Count the ladybirds' spots.
Tick the ladybird with one less spot.

Count the candles on the cakes.
Tick the cake with one more candle.

Point to each picture and count the objects.
Write the missing numbers in the boxes.

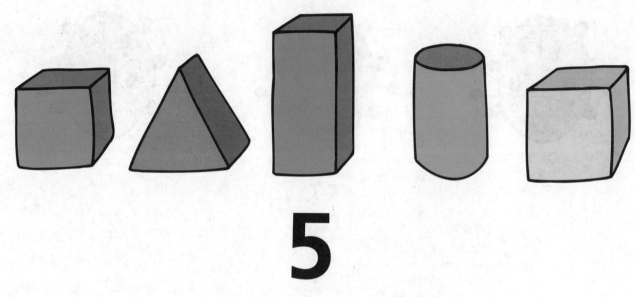

**5**

take one away leaves

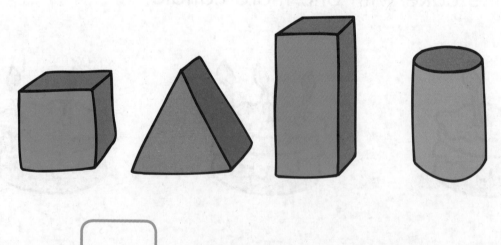

take one away leaves

Note for parent: Use real objects to practise taking away.

take one away leaves

take one away leaves

# How many are left?

Look at the picture. Pick three apples.
How many are left on the tree?
Colour them. Write your answer in the box.

Take four cakes. How many are left?
Colour it in. Write your answer in the box.

Note for parent: Activities such as these introduce your child to subtraction in a practical way.
Ask your child to cover up the required number and see how many are left.

Look at the picture. Take two crayons from the box. How many are left? Draw the answer in the box.

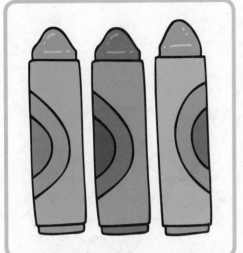

Burst two balloons. How many are left? Draw the answer in the box.

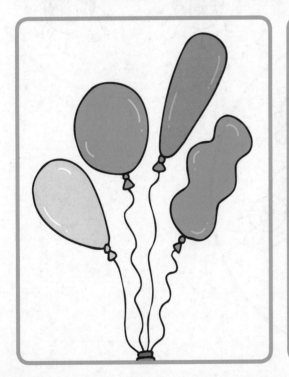

# Number groups

Count how many are in each group.

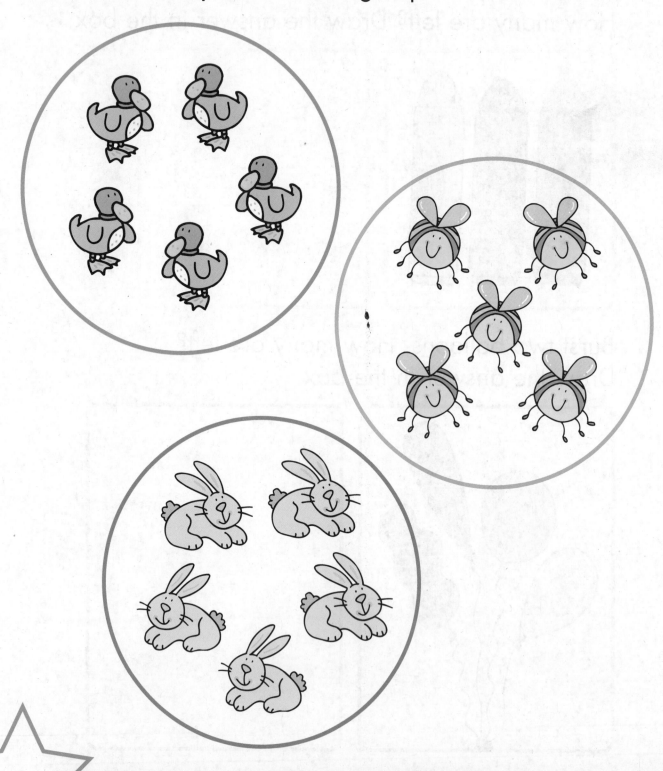

Note for parent: This activity gives further practice in counting to 5.

Tim and Sally share 6 sweets equally between them.
Draw the sweets each gets in the two groups below.

# Answers

**Page 4**

**Page 5**

**Page 6**

These people have more:

**Page 9**

1+1=2
1+1=2

**Page 10**

2+1=3

**Page 13**

more holes ✓   more dogs ✓

**Pages 14–15**

2 flags, 3 apples,
4 butterflies, 5 hats.

**Page 18**

3 shells, 4 balls, 4 presents.

**Page 20**

4 boats, 4 trees.

**Page 22**

5 stars, 5 cars.

**Page 24**

**Page 25**

☐   ✓   ☐

☐   ✓   ☐

**Pages 26–27**

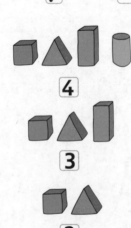

4

3

2

1

**Page 28**

2    1

**Page 29**

1 crayon is left.

2 balloons are left.

**Page 30**

5 ducks, 5 bees, 5 rabbits.

**Page 31**

Tim and Sally get 3 sweets each.

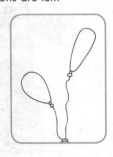

32